HAS DEMOCRACY HAD ITS DAY?

By Carl F. H. Henry

ERLC PUBLICATIONS

Published in Nashville, Tennessee,
by ERLC Publications, a subsidiary of
the Christian Life Commission
of the Southern Baptist Convention.

Cover photograph by Tom Strode
Cover design by Ernie Hickman

Henry, Carl F.H .
        Has democracy had its day?

ISBN 1-888880-00-7

Religion. Current affairs.
Library of Conbress Card Number: 96-83560

1 2 3 4 5 001 99 98 97 96

Dedication

To our son Paul
who was elected to five terms
in the U.S. Congress
and has moved to a House
built by the Carpenter of Nazareth

Contents

Introduction iii

Foreword vii

Back in Time 1

Democracy in Disorder 7

Can American Democracy Survive? 19

Reoccupying the Public Square 27

Confronting a Desacralized Culture 35

Democracy Beyond the Cold War 43

Revitalizing the Culture 51

A Resurgent Conscience 57

Introduction

Carl F. H. Henry is undeniably the twentieth century's greatest evangelical theologian, and arguably its most important theologian of any perspective. In the last decade of this turbulent and troubled century he stands head and shoulders above his contemporaries, past and present. Since the 1940s Dr. Henry has identified the issues and engaged the controversies that have been most determinative for the Christian faith. Decade after decade he has written masterfully and spoken eloquently to the most important issues confronting Christians. Surely no evangelical Christian leader has been so right so early so often on so many of the critical issues of the past half century.

Imagine my delight when I received a phone call from Dr. Henry asking whether the Christian Life Commission might be interested in publishing his latest book, entitled *Has Democracy Had Its Day?* I became increasingly excited as he described the book's thesis, and when the manuscript arrived a few days later, I read it through in one sitting. I believe *Has Democracy Had Its Day?* to be one of the most important things ever written by Dr. Henry. He brings a lifetime of insight and analysis to the question of whether a democratic society can long thrive or even continue to exist when the religious and theological underpinnings that have made such freedom possible have been abandoned. When the spiritual foundation collapses, can the implosion of the civilization which it sustained and made possible be far behind?

Has Democracy Had Its Day? is the expansion of an address given in Grand Rapids on November 7, 1995, to the Acton Institute for the Study of Religion and Liberty. The Acton Institute was named for Lord Acton, the nineteenth-century British political philosopher and historian who believed that the conscience, informed by religion and morality, was the only sufficient safeguard for freedom in civil society. How appropriate that an event sponsored by those honoring Lord Acton should provide the occasion for Dr. Henry's masterful analysis which "questions the viability of democracy apart from shared beliefs that have an anchorage deeper and higher than majority opinion" and which concludes "that only an overwhelming spiritual renewal and a massive transcendent penetration of the social order can effectively challenge and preserve a rapidly disintegrating society." All this is presented with Dr. Henry's trademark eloquence.

In *Has Democracy Had Its Day?* Dr. Henry quickly points out that while "the Bible does not commend any specific historical form as incarnating the kingdom of God, scriptural teaching on the nature of God and of human society nonetheless excludes some political options and clarifies the implications of others." He notes that "some political systems—violent liberation or chaos or totalitarian rule or absolute monarchy—are incompatible with the biblical emphasis that all humans by creation bear a divine image and are equal in worth and duty and rights." More importantly, Dr. Henry concludes that a "democratically chosen and constitutionally limited government seems to be the political structure most compatible with the Christian insistence on human worth and liberty and most likely to accommodate the promotion and protection of human freedoms, justice, and peace."

In defending democracy buttressed by the foundational truths of Judeo-Christian morality as the most promising guarantor of freedom, Dr. Henry takes on all critics, from the "Singapore School" of Far Eastern political and economic theorists to theonomist reconstructionists and neo-Marxist liberation theologians. In doing so, however, he is careful to assert that "democratic government in its highest tradition is predicated not simply on the will of the majority but looks beyond that to transcendent truth to which the political realm is accountable" and that it "views such answerability in the context of specific religious beliefs and values."

Dr. Henry, like the Old Testament's divinely appointed "watchman" (Jer. 6:17; Ezek. 3:17), sounds the warning that a moment of crisis and critical decision is at hand, both for democracy and for Judeo-Christian values as the transcendent norms for Western civilization. He not only describes and analyzes the cultural and spiritual crisis masterfully, he also confronts evangelicalism with its failure to participate in the culture as vigorously or as effectively as it could have or should have done.

Dr. Henry addressed the "uneasy conscience" of evangelicals a half century ago, challenging them to engage and penetrate an increasingly secular culture. Now, after fifty years of truly phenomenal numerical growth within evangelicalism, Dr. Henry observes that "the secular culture has impacted Evangelicals as significantly as Evangelicals have impacted the culture" and that American culture today is wretchedly worse in almost every way than the one deplored by evangelicals a half century ago. Consequently, evangelicalism itself is now in urgent need of repair and reform. This sad and tragic situation has moved evangelicalism from "an uneasy conscience" to its present "deeply unsettled spirit."

The malady that afflicts our culture could be terminal. However, Dr. Henry has rendered a brilliant, accurate, and comprehensive diagnosis. Further, he has prescribed a treatment which, if faithfully applied, will restore the patient's former health and vigor. As Dr. Henry concludes, "To exhibit again the truths and ethical absolutes of revealed religion—not least of all that Jesus Christ is 'the truth'—and define the public behavior this implies for a secular culture that has reached a moral dead end, and to do so compatibly with democratic principles, is now our demanding task."

The stakes are enormous, and the time is short. Will God's people respond? If we do not, it will not be for lack of a "watchman" who sounded the alarm and issued the call for repentance and renewal.

Richard D. Land, President
Christian Life Commission
Nashville, Tennessee

Foreword

Some fifty years ago, in the small book *The Uneasy Conscience of Modern Fundamentalism,* published by Eerdmans, I voiced a plea to then-beleaguered conservative Christians not to abandon society to the forces of Modernism, but to take a bold initiative in penetrating the social order with the biblical imperatives. The manner of that penetration was not detailed other than a call for evangelical example and persuasion rather than merely confrontation.

In the intervening years evangelical Christianity has experienced phenomenal growth. Secular humanism has dominated the cultural arena, however, in and through public education, the mass media and literature and the arts, and not least of all, the political realm. In some respects the secular culture has impacted Evangelicals as significantly as Evangelicals have impacted the culture.

This small book deals with the bearing of the contemporary culture crisis on the fortunes of democracy, the treasured political process through which voluntary religion in America and other freedoms gained an impressive cultural role. Nothing has threatened the survival of modern political democracy more than Marxist communism. One might expect that the collapse of communism in our time would evoke for democratic political processes a torrent of international tribute, yet we are seeing instead a rising tide of doubt precisely at this time.

The questioning of democracy occurs for different reasons in Latin America, in Asia, and even in Russia and Eastern Europe. But most astonishing, it appears more and more frequently in the United States, in the aftermath of the cultural loss of moral transcendence and of the privatization of religion. This book questions the viability of democracy apart from shared beliefs that have an anchorage deeper and higher than majority opinion. It also examines the recent proposals for Catholic-Evangelical cobelligerency in the political arena and discusses risks of venturing it and of neglecting it. If we are going to abandon democracy, we had better be sure of the alternative we are welcoming.

I wish to thank the Acton Institute for its invitation to present a lecture on a topic of my choice in Grand Rapids, Michigan, on November 7, 1995, and the opportunity to present these convictions in this expanded form.

Carl F. H. Henry
Watertown, Wisconsin

Back in Time

Democracy is a form of government predicated on human liberty and human equality. It involves rule by the people, either directly or representatively.

Democracy in History

When democracy first emerged in ancient Greek city-states it differed considerably from its modern expressions, and its future was problematical. In Athens, where the population numbered only about ten thousand, all citizens comprised the assembly, which acted in executive and judicial as well as legislative roles. The Greeks, moreover, sometimes elected their leaders by lot rather than by vote. Greek democracy was rather short-lived and only indirectly influenced modern theory and practice, which in form is republican or representative.

Classic Greek philosophers viewed ancient democracy critically. Socrates censured it for yielding society to leaders lacking expert knowledge and true insight; worse yet, it rated one person's opinion equally worthy to another's in respect to morality and justice. Socrates insisted that the only authentic statesmen are those who can identify the good. Plato contended that an ideal state would be ruled by an aristocracy of philosophers prepared for that task by long intellectual training. Only tyranny could be worse than majority rule, which, said Plato, would decline into rule by a despot. Aristotle, although a political relativist, viewed democracy as a deterioration from preferable forms of government; he distinguished, however, a democracy whose laws are above the people from one whose people are above law.

The Romans experimented with democracy more than

they actually implemented it. No contrast could be greater than the assumption by some pagan Roman emperors that they ruled as deities, and that of Christian Roman emperors who claimed to rule as entrusted representatives of God, unless it be the modern democratic view that government is from and by the people. The invasion of Rome put Western Europe in the service of barbarians whose terror only the combined efforts of church and state restrained.

After the breakup of the Roman Empire, almost a thousand years passed before influences that make for democracy arose again. The Magna Carta, forced on King John I in 1215, became a symbol of liberty. Some two thousand years after the Greek city-states, modern constitutionalism arose, largely influenced by medieval insistence on divine law and modern emphasis on human rights.

So-called liberal democracy, the dominant Western form, correlates the motif of popular rule with that of limited government. The divine right of kings gave way to the people's divine right to resist the absolutism of both church and state. Modern democracy is usually traced to the influence of John Locke's treatise *Of Civil Government,* which despite notable differences is thought to have inspired Jefferson's shaping of the Declaration of Independence. Locke held that in its promotion of liberty the prime purpose of government was the preservation of property. The founders designated the American nation a republic and distinguished it from a monarchy, yet the word *democracy* nowhere appears in the U.S. Constitution because some leaders had reservations about it.

Seventeenth-century England made the monarchy constitutional, but derived it from the people rather than from the deity. The principle of majority rule has increasingly become the definitive criterion of democracy. Politicians now frequently correlate constitutional government (which preserves a continuity of law through successive regimes) or limited government (which popular rule can expound in a variety of ways) with democratic processes. Despite the preferability of majority rule over minority determination, however, majority rule does not of itself assure the preservation of civil and political rights.

Constitutional government, even assuming its constraints are unqualifiedly just, does not of itself guarantee the supremacy of freedom and justice in the public order. Radical political movements are misguided when they champion majority rule as a sure door to justice and liberty. Just government can in theory prevail quite apart from majority rule. Monarchy need not be unjust; many Christians anticipate a Christocratic millennium. Majority rule, moreover, carries no assurance of limited government; it can and has been invoked in defiance of religious liberty and other rights. In time Athenian democracy unwittingly replaced oppression by a monarch with oppression by the majority. Government by the most numerous, like that by the most powerful, can fail to provide a safeguard against what Lord Acton characterized as "arbitrary revolutions of opinion" (*The History of Freedom,* Grand Rapids: The Acton Institute, 1993, p. 34).

An Age of Theocracy

It is noteworthy that Christianity stipulates no one permanent form of government in the name of divine revelation. The Hebrews, in earliest generations, were ruled directly by Yahweh, in distinction from political rule by the people. Designation of a succession of kings came later, when Israel felt a need for strong military and political leadership. They followed the pattern of neighboring nations and, over Samuel's objections, enthroned Saul about 1020 B.C. during menacing Philistine aggression. The kingdom reached its greatest power during the succession of David and then Solomon, but it fragmented after Solomon's death. The succession of Hebrew kings continued until the Babylonian conquest of Israel in 586 B.C., when Israel lost its independence and theocracy ended.

The Hebrew kings did not have legislative power; the laws were divinely given and the ruler, along with the people, was subject to God's higher law. Transcendent divine authority assured a highly limited monarchy and compatible human liberty in a world of rampant political absolutism.

3

Has Democracy Had Its Day?

The Old Testament pattern of a divine stipulation of particular regal selectees involving a covenant between Yahweh, the national ruler, and the Hebrew people apparently was unique to its time. No intimation is given that theocracy was to be revived in New Testament times or that God's people are simply to submit to divinely designated rulers. The implication is that beyond the Old Testament era the responsibility for political decision is borne by the people. This does not cancel accountability to God or leave secular theory, entirely free and unprotested, to enforce its own political forms and programs. It means rather that in the post-theocratic age political activity by believers may take a variety of forms in a predominantly Gentile society, yet remain nonetheless answerable to the justice that God stipulates.

The idea of God as king is fundamental to Judaism and Christianity. The kingdom of God is central in Jesus' teaching, where it refers not primarily to a geographical realm and its people but rather to the exercise of God's sovereign power or rule. The New Testament views all political power as a divine entrustment, accountable to the Deity for the preservation of justice and order. Jesus did not, to be sure, say to the disciples: "Go ye into all the world and teach democracy, capitalism, and privatization of business." He did not name a political apostolate. He gave priority to a gospel that sustains freedom, justice, and grace.

Yet Lord Acton reminds us pungently that when, three days before crucifixion, Jesus Christ in the temple said, "Render to God . . . render to Caesar," He set civil power in a new context: "the repudiation of absolutism and the inauguration of Freedom." To reduce political authority within defined limits "was made the perpetual charge and care of the most energetic institution and the most universal association in the world" (*The History of Freedom,* Grand Rapids: The Acton Institute, 1993, pp. 52 f.).

The end of the theocratic age does not by any means imply divine disinterest in the political realm or an abandonment of society, including the Christian community, to secular notions of public sovereignty. God never gives intellectual right-of-way to the notion that humanity defines truth and the good, or that the essential content of political philosophy is culturally conditioned and historically located. Those who deny transcendent principles of justice sooner or later will abandon the moral and political orders to chaos.

In contemporary use, democracy is a form of government in which all citizens make political decisions by acting either directly by majority rule (direct democracy), or through representatives responsible to their constituencies (representative democracy), or in which majority powers are exerted within constitutional restraints that guarantee certain minority rights also, such as freedom of speech and of religion (constitutional democracy).

Biblical Views of Political Systems

While the Bible does not commend any specific historical form as incarnating the kingdom of God, scriptural teaching on the nature of God and of human society nonetheless excludes some political options and clarifies the implications of others. With an eye on theories of law, justice, duties, and rights, Christians must interpret the political arena in the context of biblical teaching on humanity and history and society and culture.

It is evident that some political systems—violent liberation or chaos or totalitarian rule or absolute monarchy—are incompatible with the biblical emphasis that all humans by creation bear a divine image and are equal in worth and duty and rights. All members of the human community are simultaneously carriers of a created dignity and of divinely stipulated responsibilities and rights. Any political system that obscures or cancels these principles cannot be embraced as ideal. Christian duty, moreover, is personal and communal; it includes both neighbor-love and social justice (which is the form that love takes in the public order). The sovereignty of God, the Creator and Judge of all, implies the subordinate and restricted nature of human authority. Limited government is a necessary corollary of the biblical view of human freedom and responsibility; human political authority must have boundaries.

To define the proprieties of human conduct, God's transcendent will nurtures both constitutional and statute

5

law. Constitutional law assures a continuity of legal criteria throughout successive regimes. But positive law is necessary also to circumscribe the authority of human government and to protect the people from governmental abuse.

Jesus' regard for Roman authority as both legitimate and limited and Paul's references to government likewise are instructive in this regard. Jesus submitted to political authority but warned that its subordinate power was a divine entrustment. Paul taught that "the powers" are answerable to God, and himself appealed to Caesar as a divinely accountable minister of justice.

The early Christians were not zealots; if anything, except for routine law-keeping and paying taxes, they viewed Roman authority rather passively and were hesitant about military service. But this should not be said without noting that Roman emperors professed to rule by the sanction of pagan gods, that some rulers readily martyred believers, and that their policies were often predictably hostile.

It would be indefensible to translate Scripture into a declared preference for either direct or representative democracy, even if one affirms this in the context of a transcendent source and ground and acknowledges the sovereign God as Creator and Judge of all and the decisive originator of human government. Yet many Christians in the modern era consider democracy the political framework that offers superior freedom to fulfill both divine commandments and political imperatives.

The biblical emphasis on human depravity and the consequent temptation to divert political power to inordinate ends argues for limited government as least oppressive. A democratic political context appears the most promising framework for fulfilling the public duties incumbent on human beings. A democratically chosen and constitutionally limited government seems to be the political structure most compatible with the Christian insistence on human worth and liberty and most likely to accommodate the promotion and protection of human freedoms, justice, and peace.

Democracy in Disorder

Any tribute to democracy as perfect and flawless in any contemporary form misreads human nature and misvalues society and history. There is adequate justification for such present-day volumes as my own *Twilight of a Great Civilization* (Wheaton, Illinois: Crossway, 1988) and Charles Colson's *Against the Night: Living in the New Dark Ages* (Ann Arbor, Michigan: Servant Books, 1989), even if optimistic postmillennialists see the so-called contemporary culture war as but a brief aberration in the larger context of evolutionary or scientific and technological advance. The current moral and political disorder of Western society is properly deplored even by critics with no sympathy whatever for militant extremists who are inherently hostile to government.

No democratic society can forever escape the chaotic impact on family values and cultural constancy of having one birth in three out of wedlock, one out of two marriages ending in divorce, and one in three pregnancies terminated by abortion (now as routine as a hernia operation). The current prediction is that three in five of all new marriages will fail. Three and a half million unmarrieds are living together in the United States. At least half the children born in our biggest cities have no legal father. At least 135,000 Americans are living with AIDS, and more than half of these are young people. Infected mothers are birthing infected children, and many do not long outlive their babies.

Violent crime has increased fivefold in a single generation, making the United States the most violent of all the world's civilized nations. More than thirty million of our citizens fall victim to crime in a single year. Inner-city streets have become combat zones where a life may be taken for a wedding ring or a pair of sneakers.

Prisons, more numerous and more crowded than anywhere else on earth, currently incarcerate 1.5 million persons. The huge increase in the number of ex-prisoners, their families disrupted during a member's imprisonment, poses an unprecedented threat to civil order and social stability. The number of privately hired security guards now exceeds the number of public policemen.

Sporadic violence, increasingly involving teenagers with no remorse, is at times so brutal in its character and consequences that law-abiding citizens wonder whether the mindless offenders belong to the human race. Some twenty-three million people in the United States have a substance abuse problem. The peddling of "crack" and drug addiction underlies much youth violence, and police counterforces are making only a limited impact.

Sociologists speak with good reason about America's civil breakdown. The drug culture, the sexual revolution, the tailoring of morality to majority opinion, the decline of the public significance of religion, and the aggressive orientation of public schools to blatant naturalism all are features of a society inviting destruction. No nation can long preserve its own equilibrium—let alone provide world leadership—if it confuses ultimate distinctions of right and wrong and subjectivizes truth.

Alexis de Tocqueville was prophetic: "When America ceases to be good," he said, "she will also cease to be great." A society that banishes absolutes will soon ridicule guilt and shame. Many psychologists disapprove of going to bed with another's wife only if she has guilt feelings. It appears at times that everything in our culture that is moral and right is under attack. The vulgarians seem intent on destroying not only the moral law but also the transcendent source of it.

Those in the political arena may reasonably be charged as substantial contributors to the present culture crisis in the United States. The political convictions of mainstream

America mirrored in the 1992 elections reflect a belief that the nation is in moral decline and that uncertainty clouds many traditional ethical imperatives. The effort to improve political ethics collides head-on with the indifference of politicians to private immorality. Their posture poses no decisive challenge to the contemporary reduction of the meaning of "moral" to avoiding what is illegal and to doing whatever is legally tolerable. The imbalance between personal opportunity and public responsibility is seldom addressed.

A generation that elevates the essentiality of human rights to intellectual priority yet simultaneously contends that all philosophical affirmations are culture-conditioned sooner or later will engulf those very rights in moral relativism. The gathering mobs ignore others' rights while they demand not just their own rights but their personal preferences, too. The emergence of public spokesmen — including clergy — who justify as morally necessary even the deliberate murder of abortionist physicians attests the depths of ethical confusion.

In early America, town hall meetings provided a forum that gathered citizens to discuss and debate the pressing issues of the day. That precedent has given way to the incivility of rude television panels and bellicose radio talk shows. The television screen has become modernity's worship center and displaces the church as the consolidator of values. Madison Avenue promises to make everyone slim, sexy, and rich. The world of advertising is prone to view religion as a waning and dysfunctional aberration, and legitimates anything and everything but the commandments of God.

The privatization of God, the failure to harmonize racial animosities, the triumph of greed and sex over moral sense, and a deliberately confrontational spirit all are factors in American society that contribute to social breakdown and loosen democracy's life supports. It is not so much the presence of diverse views that imperils democracy, nor the existence of fiercely competing parties; it is disinterest in serious debate and the flirtation with relativism that makes the achieving of consensus elusive.

9

Democracy's Problematic Future

Despite the defeat and collapse of totalitarian powers in our century, some contemporary observers regard the future of democracy to be more and more problematical. Spared from external decimation, will democracy disintegrate, they ask, under the weight of its own internal compromises?

Only two alternatives lie before a democracy: either self-restraint and self-discipline, or chaos and authoritarian repression. James D. Hunter holds that the present social conflict over values has now become so combative that its very intensity may jeopardize American democracy (*Before the Shooting Begins: Searching for Democracy in America's Culture War,* New York: Free Press, 1994).

Angry and disaffected citizens resent their apparent inability to significantly change an entrenched and extensive government by political processes. A sense of futility over political solutions nurtures ever more aggressive protest and even violence, which must be contained if democracy is to escape serious domestic disruption.

Some extremist groups consider violence and even terrorism a legitimate democratic response in a politically unpredictable society. Their early dismissal by the media as merely a lunatic fringe overlooks the fact that their number includes soldiers routinely trained in military demolition before coming to view the government as an enemy. Some indeed are responsible members of the community and even of established churches. The political inclination to associate terrorism with Arab fundamentalists was stood on its head when the 1995 Oklahoma City disaster soon focused not upon Mideast terrorists, as in the case of the 1993 World Trade Center bombing, but rather on so-called freedom-loving Americans.

Recent events have triggered a lowered respect both for the secular media and for the criminal justice system. Conspicuous factors include the almost interminable and tragically farcical trial of 0. J. Simpson and the assault on the Branch Davidians in Waco, which some critics consider to have involved excessive force and some violation of individual rights. Some social critics now even see the

10

expansion of federal law enforcement as potentially restrictive of rights, especially in the matter of gun control.

Yet such political criticism falls well short of endorsing anti-government groups given to the demonizing of government, the stockpiling of weapons, the encouragement of rebellion, and the pursuit of express alternatives to the political process. There is assuredly no present danger of American civil war.

John Woodbridge holds that culture-war rhetoric tends to push people into competing camps rather than to the pursuit of middle ground ("Culture War Casualties," *Christianity Today,* Mar. 6, 1995, p. 23). Christians should see America, he contends, more as a mission field with a spectrum of views than as a war zone divided into a battlefield of aggressive political militants. He exhorts the churches not to embrace the pugilistic strategies of secular movements in the struggle for reform.

The secular left has sought to embarrass and silence critics on the right by characterizing aggressive radio talk shows as "hate radio." It attributes blame to Evangelicals for much of the rancor that presently exists. In his book *Uncommon Decency* (InterVarsity Press, 1992), Protestant scholar Richard Mouw holds that the inflammatory and incendiary language of Christians has contributed to the intense incivility of current public dialogue.

Yet if democracy is to survive effectively, its champions need not only to pray but also to speak up, as well as to maintain links with elected officials, and to support preferred candidates for office. Dialogue and civil political activity can still be more important than social militancy. America has remained a liberty-loving democracy for more than two hundred years because citizens were ready to stand up and be counted, and to give a reason for their position on a particular side of debate.

That democracy is in trouble is attested by a growing literature of political criticism. Christopher Lasch has written on *The Revolt of the Elites and the Betrayal of Democracy* (Norton, 1995). Jean Bethke Elshtain has written *Democracy on Trial* (Basic, 1995), and *The New*

York Times Book Review devoted a cover article (Jan. 22, 1995) to an essay with related reviews titled "Does Democracy Have a Future?" Such discussions seem all the more astonishing when viewed in the context of the global collapse of Marxism.

Democracy as a Western Villain

Some leaders, even of rapidly developing Asian nations, complain that democracy is damaging. They point to evidence that stable and economically productive Asian countries benefit most from the exertion of governmental authority in achieving ideal social prerogatives, in contrast to governmental emphasis mainly on human rights. One may contrast conditions in Singapore, for example, with the complicating stress in South Africa on black social rights in promoting economic development. Western corporations also seem all too ready to subordinate personal-rights issues when investing in Asian economies, as in mainland China, where pressure for personal rights is accommodated to a socialist market economy.

Behind these tensions lies a critically important debate over whether democracy or economics is to hold priority in the West's dealing with East Asian countries. The Singapore diplomat Kishore Mahbubani complains that Western nations, now that the Cold War is over, are prone to abandon Third World allies unless they adopt "more stringent tests of human rights and democratic rectitude" and unless they condition economic development aid on observance of these priorities ("The West and the Rest," *The National Interest,* Summer 1992, pp. 3-12). Mahbubani asks why "such accelerating demands are made in Asia when most Latin American countries receiving aid have made little progress toward democracy, or why the West does not export its higher standards, for example, to Saudi Arabia."

Many Third World observers, he comments, are concluding that the West advances democracy only when and where self-interest is involved. Promoting democracy, he says, costs the United States little, whereas economic assistance—or lack of it—may prove costly short-term or long-term.

Mahbubani and other spokesmen for what is becoming known as the "Singapore School" (which includes Singapore's elder statesmen Lee Kuan Yew and foreign affairs minister Bilahare Kausikan) profess to see in the debate over rights and/or economics a reflection of cultural differences involving Confucian and Christian (or Protestant) values. Some Western spokesmen challenge this notion, seeing it as an East Asian attempt to justify authoritarian and repressive political methods, correlated with a plea for economic assistance and the relief of human suffering as a priority. Confucian philosophy, some Western critics contend, only ambiguously responds to the agenda of mainland Chinese leaders, who seek a formula whereby the masses can better themselves economically while their rulers retain authoritarian political power. In Hong Kong one can already find, in anticipation of the 1997 turnover of power to Communist China, business tycoons who are eager for capitalism but not for an importation of Western democracy.

Still the Singapore School points to social abuses and cultural indulgences of the West as evidence of a flawed individual human rights policy that contrasts with Confucian emphasis on family values embracing both the immediate and extended family.

Lee Kuan Yew emphasizes order as a cultural *sine qua non.* He insists that the American system will not work in East Asian countries. He commends its open relationships between persons of differing social standing, ethnicity, and religion; its freedom from secrecy and terror; its outspoken argument about a good or bad society; and the accountability demanded of public officials. But in its traffic in drugs, violence, and crime he sees an erosion of the moral underpinnings of society and the diminution of personal responsibility. Westerners, he says, "have abandoned an ethical basis for society, believing that all problems are solvable by a good government" (quoted by Fareed Zakaria, "Culture Is Destiny. A Conversation with Lee Kuan Yew," *Foreign Affairs,* Vol. 73, No. 2, March/April 1994, pp. 109-194). In context, Lee's alternative somewhat mirrors a government-directed economic policy coupled with a Confucian value system with its tradition of strict discipline.

The Asian emphasis is self-reliance, says Lee, while the West's is governmental solution. The deeper issue is focused when Lee rejects the West's insistence that "all men are equal" and on "one person, one vote." People differ, he stresses, in neurological development and in cultural values. In contrast with the West's tendency to minimize and privatize religion, he notes that the rise of religion has been a phenomenon in the fast-growing East Asian countries.

Despite Lee's reservations, democratic government in its highest tradition is not predicated simply on the will of the majority but looks beyond that to transcendent truth and good to which the political realm is accountable. Moreover, it views such answerability in the context of specific religious beliefs and values.

To be sure, as David Clyde Jones observes, the United States gives no constitutional recognition to the family, in contrast to some Western democracies, despite the family's crucial role as a "mediating structure" between the individual and the state (*Biblical Christian Ethics,* Grand Rapids: Baker, 1995, p. 173). Western societies are prone to combine democracy with the notion of individual autonomy. Yet, as Peter Berger notes, Western democracies require the institutions of the family and of religion lest individualism destroy both democracy and capitalism (*The Capitalist Revolution: Fifty Propositions About Prosperity, Equality and Liberty,* New York: Basic Books, 1986). Where political leaders propose to nurture democracy contrary to the vitalities of the family and of religion they court social disaster.

Commenting on the interview with Lee, Zakaria pointedly asks: "If Confucianism explains the economic boom in East Asia today, does it not also explain that region's stagnation for four centuries?" (Zakaria, p. 125). "Many scholars," he notes, have argued that "Confucian-based cultures discouraged all the attributes necessary for success in capitalism." That Confucian culture is alien to the West is not to be doubted; whether its erosion of individual human rights offers a hopeful way into the future is a debatable proposition. Lee's criticisms of the moral decline of the West are not irrelevant. They do not establish, however, that ethical decline is integral to a democratic society.

The Korean scholar Kim Dae Jung replies to Lee's insistence that Western-style democracy is a liability inapplicable to East Asia. The defeat of communism, Kim stresses, reflected not merely a victory of capitalism over socialism, but a triumph also of democracy over dictatorship. The moral breakdown of Western societies, Kim insists, is not due "to too much democracy and too many individual rights," nor merely to reliance on government, for the government in Singapore and in other Eastern Asian countries "stringently regulates individual actions" to "an Orwellian extreme of social engineering." Moral deterioration, Kim notes, is common to industrial societies, and East Asian countries are not exempt from it ("Is Culture Destiny?" *Foreign Affairs,* Vol. 73, No. 6, November/ December 1994, pp. 189-194).

Eric Jones, an Australian professor of economic history, further protests that the Asian alternative implies the idea of mass prosperity amid a muzzled press, arbitrary arrest, forced labor, and public executions; representative government and individual freedoms are excluded ("Asia's Fate: A Response to the Singapore School," *The National Interest,* Spring 1994, pp. 18-28). He notes that the Singapore School has not demonstrated what is elsewhere evident, that economic growth is compatible with democracy and more individual rights.

The wrongs of the West, Jones stresses, do not justify the wrongs of East Asia. While authoritarian government has in recent years delivered economic growth, it "almost never did so" during the Confucian era. Individual freedom has nurtured originality and novelty. Moreover, "orderly succession is nowhere as satisfactorily guaranteed as in Western parliamentary democracies." Furthermore, he speaks of a latent universal demand for democracy and individual freedoms. The use of undemocratic means to achieve desirable ends may leave human beings richer in everything but freedom. The delivery of material well-being need not permanently inure East Asians to political authoritarianism.

For all that, Jones, although a champion of representative democracy, thinks we must answer "'almost certainly not' or even 'a flat no' to the question whether East and Southeast Asia will become recognizably democratic within the next five or ten years." Given a generation, he is "more hopeful" that a new middle class will ultimately transform the prevailing East Asian social and political reality.

David Martin Jones of the National University of Singapore replies that the rapid and sustained growth of the East Asian countries has more to do with the shrewd planning of post-colonial rulers than with a growth of democratic ideas.

Alan Wisdom, vice president of The Institute on Religion and Democracy, scores an important point pertaining to the criticism of liberal democracy by Asian leaders and by others of authoritarian disposition in other parts of the world who reject democracy in practice. "To contest democracy in theory," Wisdom says, "requires a confidence that one knows alternative forms of social organization that can claim to be more just. It is that confidence that the Asian authoritarians apparently possess."

Theonomists and Liberationists

A similar confidence is expounded in a very different direction by a small but vocal cadre of American theonomists or reconstructionists, who view democracy more or less as a heretical option and insist that Mosaic law in its entirety is universally and timelessly valid. In a strikingly different way, Muslim fundamentalists in the Middle East champion absolute Islamic authority and strenuously oppose moderates who hold that the Koran and democracy can be reconciled.

Theonomists consider democracy a lamentable defection from and capitulation of the biblical tradition to its historic Greco-Roman rival. Theonomists hold that Christians living in a democracy should persuade all citizens to live by Mosaic law.

The issue here at stake is not whether every earthly sovereignty is ideally subordinate to the sovereignty of Jesus

Christ, for the final consummation of the rule of Christ remains a universal Christian hope.

Evangelical critics of theonomists remain unpersuaded that the New Testament imposes theonomous government upon the political arena in the name of Christian duty. David Clyde Jones rightly stresses that the church as a covenant community is not now coextensive with the nation as it was in ancient Israel (*Biblical Christian Ethics,* Grand Rapids: Baker, 1995, p. 115). It is only the regenerate community within the larger social and political order that may be expected now to exist in theocratic or Christocentric relationships that ultimately will govern all nations and races of humanity. Such end-time rule by the Risen Lord, however, need not presuppose the unacceptability of democracy as an interim political order embracing religious liberty.

Not a few Latin American spokesmen consider democratic regimes too weak to achieve necessary structural changes; such regimes are simply postponing the day when more aggressive reform movements relying on authoritarian methods take over. Kim Dae Jung notes, however, that "the many Latin American states that in recent decades embraced capitalism while rejecting democracy failed miserably. On the other hand, countries practicing democratic capitalism or democratic socialism, despite temporary setbacks, have prospered" ("Is Culture Destiny?" *Foreign Affairs,* Vol. 73, No. 6, November/December 1994, p. 189). Small but powerful elites poised to intervene are prone to minimize erstwhile limited democratic successes in Columbia, Costa Rica, Mexico, and Venezuela. The replacement of dictatorial regimes and corrupt political institutions and structures requires much patience.

Shrill criticism of democracy has been voiced by Marxist-prone revolutionary theologians who consider education, legislation, and even regeneration too slow a means of major social change and rely instead on force. They often appeal to the Hebrew exodus from Egypt as a paradigm, although the Hebrews never even intended to demolish the Egyptians, nor did they impose on them a different form of government.

Can American Democracy Survive?

It is specifically American democracy—long the envy of much of the modern world—whose political fortunes are now in question. Bruce D. Porter asks, "Can American Democracy Survive?" and points to centrifugal forces that "are tearing at the fabric of American society" (*Commentary*, Vol. 96, No. 5, Nov. 1993, pp. 37-40). In much the same spirit, Os Guinness comments that despite the international victory for America's political and economic order, the nation's present moral and cultural turmoil renders questionable "whether America's cultural order is capable of nourishing the freedom, responsibility, and civility that Americans require to sustain democracy" (*Dining with the Devil: The Megachurch Movement Flirts with Modernity*, Grand Rapids: Baker, 1993, p. 165).

The mounting cynicism and contempt with which some of the nation's most influential institutions are sporadically viewed—the presidency, controversial cabinet officials, the CIA, members of Congress involved in scandal and corruption, even military misjudgment and misinformation—reflect periodic doubt that the rule of law will prevail. The call for political change comes, remarkably, even from those who have benefited from government programs, but who see the burden of taxation as a hindrance to their effective participation in the American dream. Their declining confidence in federal government focuses on

19

wasteful spending and a failure to control budget deficits.

This mood of open criticism rises more and more frequently from a generation but a few decades removed from a day when officeholders were expected to adhere to ethical standards exemplary for the entire citizenry and in which presidents were commended for using their "bully pulpit" to exhort the general populace to act on the highest motives.

What the American masses currently fear is lack of national direction and political purpose. Some radicals have argued that freedom entitles individuals to choose their own political values and that it is coercive to confront them with democratic options. But this veiled promotion of Marxism, supposedly in the name of freedom, exalts a political theory that would in effect strip away humanity's freedom of choice and whose champions have not hesitated to imprison critics of a ruling party.

In his classic work on *Democracy in America* (1835-1840), Tocqueville noted that the benefits of "democracy" impressively surprise the foreigner who comes to the United States. Writing a century and a half later, Lasch observes that "violence, crime, and general disorder almost invariably strike foreign visitors as the most salient features of American life" (*Revolt of the Elites,* p. 213).

Lasch recites as signs of "the impending collapse of social order" (Ibid., p. 213) concerns that sociologists now routinely report: widespread lust for immediate gratification, pursuit of inordinate self-interest, self-fulfillment and self-esteem, recruitment of young children into the culture of crime, and pervasive defection from standards of behavior that "once were considered indispensable to democracy" (Ibid., p. 215). Surely one might add that the moral vagrancy of a generation that has aborted some 1.5 million fetuses in a single year predictably breeds a society that believes human existence is suspended merely on another's preference. The shamelessness of secular society is all the more deplorable in elitist manifestations that embody bold immodesty and moral rebellion.

The term *democracy* was viewed with disdain when it came into general political use at the end of the eighteenth century. Some political theorists deplored it as the worst of all options. To them the designation suggested violent and uncontrollable mobs. The first two goals of the French Revolution—equality and freedom—were considered incompatible. This mood still prevailed in Europe when Tocqueville visited the United States. Tocqueville himself held that the democratic premise of equality undervalued superior achievement while advancing the preservation of liberty as a nation's prime task. All considerations were subordinated to a vote of the majority, a principle that threatened to debase not only sociopolitical life but all cultural values.

If ever America's free institutions are destroyed, predicted Tocqueville, "that event may be attributed to the omnicompetence of the majority, which may at some future time urge the minorities to desperation and oblige them to have recourse to physical force. Anarchy will then be the result, but it will have been brought about by despotism" (*Democracy in America,* Phillips Bradley edition, Vintage Books, I, p. 279). Tocqueville clearly considered the strength of the majority inadequate to retard tyranny.

The Loss of Moral Transcendence

Lasch contends that it is not mass culture but rather the cultural elite who now comprise the center of moral and cultural rebellion against the spiritual and ethical heritage of the West. They, more than the masses, have contributed to "the gradual decay of religion" as a formative public influence and to the worsening absence of internal constraints essential to the survival of a democracy (*Revolt of the Elites,* p. 215).

Tocqueville maintained that religion, as a basic part of human nature, helps powerfully to maintain republican institutions. "Men cannot abandon their religious faith without a kind of aberration of intellect," he wrote (*op. cit.,* I 310). Even the nonreligious feed on the very creeds they have rejected.

At the same time, Tocqueville was an ardent champion of church-state separation. Reared a Catholic, he was devoutly religious, though he is depicted often as less a practitioner than a believer. Tocqueville urged that the lessons of religiopolitical struggle in Europe not be ignored. "In Europe," he writes, "Christianity has been intimately united to the powers of the earth. These powers are now in decay.... The living body of religion has been bound down to a dead corpse of superannuated polity" (Ibid., I, 314).

Tocqueville acknowledged that the key to religion's peaceful role in the United States lies in the rule of church-state separation (Ibid., I, 308). The clergy deliberately abstain from politics, he commented, and public opinion excludes them from political appointments (Ibid., I, 309). The clergy would surrender their religious influence if they strove for political power (Ibid., I, 312). "In proportion as a nation assumes a democratic condition of societies and as communities display democratic propensities, it becomes more and more dangerous to connect religion with political institutions" (Ibid., I, 311).

During the twentieth century, communism, the global enemy of democracy, was dedicated to absolute church-state separation. More accurately, communist state absolutism was devoted to the control, decimation, and destruction of the churches.

The supreme incongruity of the Soviet empire's collapse, and perhaps the most remarkable consequence of the disintegration of communism, is the agitation and disorientation this turn of events has thrust upon the Western democracies. John Gray has put the matter pointedly: "Deprived of the easy certainties of the cold war, they have entered the post-Communist period less confident about their basic institutions and values than at any time since the end of Word War II.... In the United States the end of the cold war has intensified a mood of public cynicism. American public opinion expects little from its democratic institutions" (*The New York Times Book Review, op. cit.*, p. 1).

Democratic society now contends with staggering new problems. Among domestic concerns, we may note: the malevolence of violent terrorists in a free and open society; the dislocation of hundreds of thousands of jobless who are unqualified for work in the information age; the skill of highly salaried defense lawyers in protecting the interests of powerful lobbies and in influencing juries or achieving mistrials in cases involving monied clients or large corporations; political campaign costs that compel presidential candidates to raise $15 to $20 million; and radical feminism which dismisses the entire history of the West as predicated on patriarchal prejudices that invalidate its governing ideals.

It is proper for a sociologist or journalist to comment with alarm on the decline of the Western democracies, for the current critique of democracy reflects some of our century's most destructive forces. But a Christian theologian or philosopher needs to indicate also what may and must be done to arrest that decline and if possible to reverse it.

The Necessity of Participation

Indicating the superiority of the democratic option and the necessity and possibility of its reformation and preservation is among our generation's highest priorities. Lasch remarks incisively that "the office of the devoted teacher is not to deify or even defend a 'dying culture' but to resist the 'downward identification' that threatens any form of culture at all" (*op. cit.*, p. 221). In an age when accepted standards of right and wrong are scorned, when absolutes are demeaned as a return to the superseded past, when doubt threatens to evaporate great national beliefs and political principles and weakens inherited guidelines, when new conceptions degrade the minds and corrupt the lives of the newly emerging generations, those who refuse to abandon history to the forces of decadence must speak out.

The question is earnestly raised whether a continuing indifference of citizens to political involvement (only 55.9 percent of the voting-age population went to the polls in the 1992 presidential election) might not allow democracy simply to dwindle into inconsequence. Many Americans are losing touch with national ideals. Democracy can be forfeited if the people neglect intelligent participation in public affairs and if they elevate personal ambition over civic justice. Proposals for reinventing citizenship are therefore not irrelevant; nor are those for a recovery of volunteerism, neighbor-responsibility, and neighbor-love.

Not to be personally engaged in this time of cultural indecision and moral confusion is to be unworthy not only of democratic political existence, but of significant human survival as well. Granted that Soviet missiles and warheads no longer point toward Washington, meaningful survival depends on much more than a repression of international terrorism and the establishment of tenuous world peace. Political stability will not be assured simply by retaining "democracy" as a civilizational password.

Evangelical participation in public affairs too often has displayed a role of confrontation rather than penetration, an overarching mood of resentment more than democratic participation. The town-hall spirit of public debate amid respect for the personal dignity of all citizens has at times deteriorated to sheer rivalry and animosity between competing movements. No society can long survive without respect for the rights of its members and some contribution by its members toward its maintenance.

The nation has a much bigger bill to pay than a paralyzing budget imbalance; it must face the cost of defection from the Deity. A religious belief compatible with the goals of society—such as the doctrine of universal divine judgment—can condition social behavior more than totalitarian coercion, enlightened self-interest, and a merely secular belief that one should respect the rights of others.

Christopher Wolfe rightly shares Tocqueville's belief that a virile democracy requires the reinforcement of religion *(Essays on Faith and Liberal Democracy,* Lanham, Maryland: University Press of America, 1987, p. 59). The declining influence of religion in national life erodes the virility of democracy. But what religious emphases are essential or contributory to the well-being of democracy? Wolfe holds that Christianity is true, especially its Catholic form, and that it promotes democratic tendencies that exceed what politics by itself can supply (Ibid., p. 66; cf. p. 2).

Each of these premises has its critical respondents in American society. But fundamental questions intrude: Is democracy damaging to true religion, and is democracy compatible with a Christian view of society? Behind the issue of religion's importance in society and in political affairs lies the companion concern over the importance of truth in public religion.

A Proposal to Withdraw

Thomas Molnar, internationally known Roman Catholic layman and author of many books, deplores democracy as largely a Protestant liberal innovation. He proposes that, instead of engaging in the political process on the assumptions of a pluralistic society, the church should withdraw and seek a renewal of culture on her own premises. Molnar contends that the weakening of royal authority by the Protestant Reformers "prepared the way for...the concept of popular sovereignty and for democracy" (Thomas Molnar, *Utopia, the Perennial Heresy,* New York: Sheed and Ward, 1967, p. 171).

"At first...church and state represented two aspects of the unified and immutable cosmic-divine order perceived in Christ's revelation" (Thomas Molnar, *Twin Powers: Politics and the Sacred,* Grand Rapids: Eerdmans, 1988, p. 77). But the human political community no longer recognizes any transcendent affiliation. The rules of democracy come from individual consciousness without transcendent reference; only private relationships to God survive (Ibid., p. 95). The democratic society, which the United States exemplifies, has no arbiter other than self-interest (Ibid., p. 103).

Molnar disowns John Courtney Murray's effort to reconcile democracy with the traditional emphasis on a transcendent affiliation, since Murray "had to legitimize by religious standards a political construct born in a Deistic-agnostic age and conceived by men who were clearly stamped by Enlightenment ideology, including the Masonic doctrine" (Ibid., pp. 106 f.). Democracy is not founded on the sacred but needs a substitute for it. According to Murray, this is provided intellectually by the speculative affirmation of self-evident truths.

But in a pluralistic society, Molnar insists, lack of consensus leads to discord and anarchy. Secular humanists dissent from a semireligious reference and propose their own civic theology (Ibid., p. 110). American society deviates from a long tradition that considered political power inseparable from spiritual authority (Ibid., p. 111). Liberal democracy comprises "the passage from society founded on the sacred to society founded on nothing but itself" (Ibid, p. 116). The grand error of contemporary thinkers, he says, is to "devise a political and social order without the sacred component" (Ibid., p. 128). Whereas in the past the presence of God was involved in the political hierarchy and the law-giving process, the abolition of extra-mundane meaning is now concealed by equating freedom with the secular media and a consumer mentality (Ibid., p. 118).

Reoccupying
the Public Square

This conviction that the survival of America is rendered problematical by "the naked public square," that is, the desacralization of society, is fully shared by Richard John Neuhaus, onetime Lutheran (Missouri Synod) pastor, subsequently ordained to the Roman Catholic priesthood, and a prolific writer. The scope of religion has been narrowed, Neuhaus protests, to the lone ideal of freedom—not, moreover, primarily as a means of attaining worthy goals but as itself the social objective. Religion has been tapered to a matter of individual privacy. Yet in the absence of a transcendent arbiter neither a morally good life nor ethical social ends can be validated.

Neuhaus declares this a strategic opportunity, indeed "the Catholic moment," for shaping a sociopolitical reversal: "This can and should be the moment in which the Roman Catholic Church in the United States assumes its rightful role in the culture-forming task of constructing a religiously informed public philosophy for the American experiment of ordered liberty" (*The Catholic Moment: The Paradox of the Church in the Postmodern World,* San Francisco: Harper & Row, 1987).

To reclothe the naked public square Neuhaus emphasizes the political importance of traditional moral and religious values. He has taken a formative role in shaping think tanks such as The Institute on Religion and Democracy, Ethics and Public Policy Center, The Institute on Religion and Public Life, and the monthly journal *First Things.*

Neuhaus does not, as some are prone, regard American

27

democratic governance as a Protestant heresy. He contends that Catholic teaching "incorporates" it theologically and philosophically. This is best evidenced, Neuhaus indicates, by John Paul II's 1991 papal encyclical *Centisimus Annus.* While Protestantism played "a critical role," the encyclical, says Neuhaus, firmly grounds the constituting ideas of democracy in Catholic tradition, including Scripture and the church fathers.

In *The Naked Public Square* (Grand Rapids: Eerdmans, 1984) Neuhaus declares democracy "the appropriate form of governance in a fallen creation in which no person or institution, including the Church, can infallibly speak for God."

As an alternative to both religious withdrawal from politics and religious legislative coercion, Neuhaus calls for the reconstruction of a public philosophy of religiously based values to be persuasively articulated in the currently "naked" public square in the direction of a perpetuation of Judeo-Christian ideals. Neuhaus emphasizes that democracy thrives best when transcendent truth and good are recognized. He considers portrayal of the United States as a wholly secular society unjustifiable and inaccurate, because moral and religious judgments are inescapable. All efforts to completely secularize the nation are doomed because some value system is implicit in all thought and action.

Neuhaus views the emergence of the new Christian right as a response to federal intrusion into the realm of religious values and as a contribution to morally responsible democracy. As the method of political change Neuhaus commends persuasion, not coercion, but if it is to be successful, this calls for a shared political philosophy and strategy. A veteran political activist long involved in liberal social issues, he found conservative Evangelicals quite unsophisticated in the analysis of the philosophical nuances of democracy, although they held a firm view of divine providence and were ready to engage in political concerns.

The Moral Majority, launched by Jerry Falwell, forged a link between conservative Catholics and fundamentalist Protestants who resisted the federal government's intrusion into the sphere of religious values, notably the virtual elimination of school prayer and the public funding of abortion. The Religious Right gave cultural identity to an impressively large voting bloc of citizens committed to Judeo-Christian values, although it did not achieve passage of any of its specific legislative proposals. Neuhaus has forged larger alliances embracing conservative ecumenical Protestants. Most recently he has shepherded a statement by Evangelical and Catholic leaders aimed at halting the secular humanist erosion of Judeo-Christian values and promoting a cooperative sociopolitical framework for the reinvigoration of democracy and for cultural renewal.

Neuhaus' seizure of "the Catholic moment" has drawn fire on both religious and political grounds. The proposal for Evangelical-Catholic cobelligerency displeased many Reformation Protestants who thought it dwarfed the main theological issues historically separating Rome and the Reformers. But no less significant was the charge by some Catholic intellectuals, most notably Molnar, that the Neuhaus thrust inexcusably promotes an unacceptable political philosophy—liberal democracy—that condemns the Christian option to existing as but one among many alternatives, while subscribing uncritically to church-state separation.

Molnar denies that the church is indebted to modern Western concepts for the political emphasis on human equality and inalienable rights (*Ecumenism or New Reformation,* New York: Funk & Wagnalls, 1968, p. 88) or that the church needs to update her traditions by modern democratic procedures (Ibid., p. 138). He challenges the notion that fidelity to God requires sociopolitical commitments akin to "democracy, pluralism, and the rule of the common citizen" (*Twin Powers,* p. 106). He criticizes Neuhaus for seeking "a substitute sacred" that would be compatible "with the primacy of the pluralist status quo" rather than a "rededication to the sacred" (Ibid., p. 132).

Church and State Revisited

Molnar asks rhetorically whether the apostle Peter's authority stopped "at the gates of heaven" or whether "Peter's descendants, the popes" have implicitly the right to judge and depose rulers who endangered their subjects' salvation (*The Decline of the Intellectual,* New Rochelle, N.Y.: Arlington House, 1973, p. 21). Separation of church and state, writes Molnar, was "a historic catastrophe" (*The Church, Pilgrim of Centuries,* Grand Rapids: Eerdmans, 1990, p. 145, n. 10). Modern church-state separation toppled the church from its central influence into but a corner of pluralistic society and destined it to become merely one interest group among many (Ibid., p. 3). The church is free to live at distinct disadvantage in "a milieu subtly determined by secular humanism" (Ibid., p. 5).

"When in the West Christ and Caesar shared power they shared agreement also that no society can survive without a moral substratum.... Today entire societies, including state and church, may suffer the loss of moral conscience" (Ibid., p. 148). "Liberal democracy, built on the premise of a limitless increase of human rights..., is the most fragile construct in the history of human achievements. It may not outlive this century" (Ibid., p. 144).

If Molnar does not consider democracy simply a Protestant Anglo-Saxon innovation it is only because it is anticipated in Cicero's thought and in the communes of the Middle Ages, even though its pluralistic excrescence is essentially American. Molnar's critique is mainly Platonic: Once democracy becomes the driving nucleus of polity, spiritual/intellectual life is impoverished and all institutions collapse one after the other for lack of cohesive authority.

Molnar deplores the gradual acquisition of political hegemony by civil society within the framework of the Western nations during the last four centuries ("The Liberal Hegemony: The Rise of Civil Society," in *The Intercollegiate Review,* Spring, 1994, pp. 7-16, p. 11). The church here declares for religious pluralism, he protests, "curbs its mission to convert,... retreats on educational matters, democratizes itself" (Ibid., p. 14). A near-ideal alternative, proposes Molnar (as "a solid anti-democrat") would be the mixed regime of state, church, and civil society, with none possessing the hegemony. This would at least surmount the risk involved in "the hegemony of any one component" (Ibid. p. 15).

Although Molnar dismisses both pluralistic liberal-democracy and socialist-Marxist options as unpromising, he does not propose a return to church-state alliance, which evolved from the special situation of Constantine's conversion and the Roman Empire's collapse. He considers the restoration of Christendom a delusory hope, at least for the foreseeable future. Instead, the pilgrim church must forego politics for respiritualization that focuses on the gospel more than on social services. While the church cannot entirely forego the reshaping of civilization, neither can it simply recreate structures of the past.

Molnar's insistence that the institution of the papacy gives absolute certainty in matters of faith and morals is jeopardized by his own complaint that the church's conciliar documents are read in a variety of ways. The doctrinal ambiguity that he attributes to the contemporary church clouds the prospect of decisive spiritual and cultural renewal. With the end of the Second Vatican Council in 1965 and its updating of the Roman church, says Molnar, came the church's decline from the center to the margin of ethical discourse, to become just one among many moral compasses expressing a conformist democratic mind-set. As a result, he warns, the church is on the way to irrelevance and extinction. Molnar's Roman Catholic critics reply that Christ's assurance that the gates of hell will not prevail against the church and the magisterium precludes both irrelevance and extinction.

Molnar complains that the U.S. Constitution neutralizes the Catholic Church from a leading role associated with public power (Ibid. p. 109). Neuhaus' thesis therefore is doubly utopian in its call "for the church to fill the vacuum with a supraeconomic, public political philosophy, religiously informed and culturally creative" (Ibid., p. 110). This is to be achieved—satirizes Molnar—through Christian ecumenism, in dialogue with other Christians, moralizing America "by injecting doses of Christian morality into its shabby and tattered public doctrine" (Ibid., pp. 110 f.). This proposal "sees the temporal salvation of America as a consequence of ecumenism [or] a restated pluralism" (Ibid., p. 111).

The church would in that case remain "a mere interest group" vis-a-vis secular society, Molnar protests (Ibid., p.

112). He shares the view of Tocqueville and of Lord Acton that individualism and pluralism will disrupt any society in which Catholic doctrine and ethics are not preponderantly active, and that a religiously informed public philosophy would be unnecessary were the nation ordered by more traditional church-state patterns (Ibid, p. 109).

"Political society and public policy in modern times are founded on the presupposition that since there is no truth no participant may claim to possess it" (Ibid, p. 69). 'The church must retrace her steps and go behind the loss of political power and of territorial power, maintain doctrinal fidelity, and occupy a new place in the world" (Ibid., p. 119). "Its task is not that of restoring Europe (or the West) to Christian culture" (Ibid., p. 131). Its central vocation is a theology of mission rather than liberation (Ibid., p. 140).

Politics is not thereby excluded as evil, but it is to be pursued on very different premises than those of Jacques Maritain, John Courtney Murray, and Richard John Neuhaus. Liberalism, says Molnar, became "the accepted ideal in its proposal of a new, hardly Catholic definition of morality and the common good" (Ibid., p. 7). Yet Maritain and then Murray viewed liberal democracy as the regime— in Molnar's words—"closest to what a Christian civilization may produce in the temporal order of things" (Ibid, p. 20). Molnar questions the thesis that the church, separated from the state, "would automatically find a shelter under the vast dome of civil society, and that, in turn, it would stand by as society's guardian in moral matters and as a decent public society." What if liberalism, and modernity in general, he asks, "remained hostile to the Church" and continued to regard the church "as both an anachronism and an irritant" (Ibid., p. 21)?

While Neuhaus proclaims "the Catholic moment," Molnar affirms that "the Catholic church alone" is potentially positioned to create a new culture because "it alone in the West has kept the cult alive even among doubts, tribulations, and cultural ruin" (Ibid., p. 168). The church's present humiliation justifies "the church's withdrawal from 'politics' and her renewal instead of the missionary task and the shaping of culture" (Ibid., p. 172).

Church-state separation linked the church with civil society, "a master harsher than the state" (Ibid., p. 173), one that neutralized and marginalized the Christian religion and "replaced it with a godless and immoral ideology that has become unstated and unwritten, but all-pervasively— the real and effective creed of most regimes in the West" (Ibid., p. 174). In accord with this, Neuhaus, contends Molnar, seeks not the indispensably transcendent sacred, but "a formula by which individuals and society as a whole could perform their traditional functions without the sacred" (Ibid., p. 132).

Confronting a Desacralized Culture

Modernity sought to lay the groundwork of a profane and desacralized "humanist culture—the first secular culture in history—and it has failed; civil society today lives off the past" (Molnar, *Twin Powers*, p. 170). Instead of being essentially pluralistic and thereby guaranteeing freedom, it emphasizes individual rights and desires rather than corporate responsibility, and relativizes truth and the good. The liberal vision is one-dimensional; it ignores divine providence in history (Ibid., p. 175). A political consciousness replaces the spiritual. Molnar foresees the decline of liberalism, although he is ambiguous about the near-term historical. He asks whether community can exist in the absence of a sacred component and "by the mere power of rational decisions and intellectual discourse" (Ibid, p. 137). His reply is: "All we can say is that we do not know, since we have never before tried" (Ibid., p. 138).

Neuhaus is unwilling to yield to secular humanism its ongoing erosion of Judeo-Christian cultural values. Neuhaus considers liberal democracy a preferable political system given the pluralistic context of modern life. Although he has not publicly developed the ontological foundations of his political agenda, Neuhaus relates to a network of Catholic scholars whose overall emphasis is compatible with the Thomist insistence on natural law not bound to divine revelation but supposedly deducible from human reason and congruous also with a political strategy emphasizing the "common good," as did Murray earlier in this generation.

If Molnar classifies Neuhaus with social critics who attempt to circumvent the transcendent sacred and who regard only the authority of the citizens' freedom and judgment as sufficient for the ordering of political existence, it must be noted that Neuhaus has devoted increasing emphasis not merely to the "Moral Majority" but also to specifically Judeo-Christian values as a basis of Evangelical-Catholic political cobelligerency in a cultural arena which is now conspicuously dominated by secular humanism. As theological commonalities are stressed, however, tensions arise on both the Evangelical and Catholic right, while the question of political strategy and objectives tends to call for a clearer explication of political philosophy. Most Evangelicals are wary of natural law theory (which no longer is taught even in many law schools), whereas Catholic commitment to natural law is still widespread. The interfaith cultural alliance is fraught with other uncertainties. Evangelicals have no shared political philosophy, a vacuum that Catholic philosophers would eagerly fill.

Molnar is doubtless right, that a genuinely Christian political philosophy would include ancient ecumenical creedal commitments, although the question remains whether Christian ethics will be politically imposed upon society or whether its fortunes turn solely on evangelism and religious voluntarism. Molnar's emphasis seems to call for immediate and open exposition of the sacred in terms of normative Catholic theology and cultural engagement on explicitly Catholic terms, including the papal Catholicism of Thomas Aquinas. In the absence of this, Molnar foresees only "short-lived arrangements" which find no adequate support in the residual sacred alongside modern individualism (Ibid., p. 138).

To redefine a nation's central inspiration and foundation with every new generation, insists Molnar, does not escape the individualism that "today is responsible for the fragility of Western societies and their miscomprehension of power" (Ibid., p. 112). The state formerly commanded respect

36

because it acknowledged its sacred origins; a nonsacralized power cannot long function once its promises are found to be illusory. The modern alternatives to the Christian world view and to the transcendent sacred are a mechanical universe and the demigod of technology, the negators of morality and of the soul. The marginalization, irrelevance, and decline of the church are implicit in alliances with a secular elite that cherishes laws that clash head-on with Christian morality.

Molnar has no interest whatever in an ecumenism that multiplies the possibilities of moral impact on the political arena, least of all when the framework of proposed penetration is that of a pluralistic society. Ecumenism, he says, is "a game that intellectuals play" (Ibid., p. 143). The church should rather pursue respiritualization at the expense of politics (Ibid., p. 145).

The American Evangelical community is thus confronted by a remarkable set of options and alternatives precisely at the point where it has reentered the political arena aggressively after two generations of withdrawal and hesitancy. On the one hand it has revived the danger of looking to politics as the ideal catalyst for social change, an engagement that some Evangelicals energetically venture on the political right much as liberal Protestant ecumenists a generation ago ventured it on the left in the form of the Social Gospel. At the same time, some see this engagement in terms of the rescue of Western culture. To such religious forces Molnar's warning is pointed: A new spiritual and moral focus for the church will be aware of the bankruptcy of the West and of the potential of the non-West, even as during the decline of the Roman Empire barbarian Europe was providentially open to penetration. "A Christian culture no longer exists in the West," remarks Molnar, and "restoration is a praiseworthy but unrealistic attempt" (Ibid., p. 154). Cultures do not arise or revive through a planned strategy nor is it imposed from the outside (Ibid., pp. 160 f.); it is a by-product of truth and trust and the church's mediatorial function (Ibid., p. 164). The doom of Western culture is not inevitable, but its escape from doom is far from assured.

The spiritual impoverishment of American culture is a theme echoed by Alasdair MacIntyre's *After Virtue* (1981) and by Alan Bloom's *The Closing of the American Mind* (1987) and by a growing number of social assessments. But Molnar sharply critiques American democracy as comprising an essentially desacralized society whose citizens are but equal parts of a mechanism in which material goods are humanity's main satisfaction. Consequently, Molnar understandably deplores both Murray's effort to Americanize Catholicism and Neuhaus' endorsement of a liberal democracy.

As a portrayal of America as a whole, however, Molnar's criticisms are somewhat overstated. He ignores significant manifestations of devout spirituality and of political idealism. Although in contemporary context the sacred seems to multitudes no longer credible, by no means has all modernity lost the transcendent. Molnar overstates the vices of American democracy and understates the abominations of the Middle Ages. Amid references to monarchial polity nothing is said about the arrogance of medieval kings and popes or about the terrors of the Inquisition, and little is said about freedom except in a negative way. There is scarcely a word about the remarkable Evangelical resurgence that in contemporary America has virtually displaced the Protestant mainline and has attracted even many Catholics—even if its cultural impact has been limited by the lack of a shared public philosophy.

A Call to Engagement

On the other hand, Neuhaus' call for political engagement, primarily to halt the erosion of Judeo-Christian values and to advance political positions that preserve for the Christian community the public benefits available to others, is a legitimate and necessary program. Christians are citizens of two worlds, and the high price of neglect of cultural and political participation is that secular humanism or some other costly alternative will dominate the field. To the extent that Christians are able and competent they must, if they are not to penalize themselves, actively participate in the political process.

But any revocation of church-state separation would likely unleash a costly politicizing of religious forces, even as would its preservation if developed along deliberately atheistic lines. Only a church that carefully balances both spiritual mission and political participation can serve well the interests both of its Lord and a democratic society. The adequacy of proposals for religious freedom and for pursuit of a "common good," and the legitimacy of claims for natural law and for a creation-ethic and their insistence on a law higher than even the will of the majority, are inevitable aspects of political discussion in a society that insists on human dignity.

In recent decades theologians and churchmen have shown a growing disposition to move beyond the traditional emphasis that the Christian church ideally promotes the betterment of the world only by engaging in personal evangelistic conversion. They also have moved beyond an institution that merely identifies and proclaims biblical social principles, which the laity as leaven in society are urged to apply by formulating answers to specific sociopolitical problems.

What increasingly has emerged is an expanded view of the church's role in concrete political matters. The National Council of Churches and the U. S. Catholic Conference have repeatedly sponsored specific political positions on numerous issues. Whether or not such bodies speak authoritatively for the church, their pronouncements carry the prestige of official statements; contrary opinions would by implication seem to offer false options. If such ecumenical pronouncements are wrong, the public understandably attributes erroneous speculation to the church. In brief, the ascription of ecclesiastical authority to essentially human opinion can serve to discredit the church.

The usual rejoinder is that without an espousal of specific positions the church's social impact is nil. But the notion that the ecumenical adoption of specific pronouncements has a transforming social effect is illusory. The laity often have more technical expertise than the clergy, yet their achievements remain limited. Moreover, the church has no assurance that its political action can overcome the flaws of political institutions. The imperative love of God and of neighbor have better prospect of altering the sociopolitical arena.

This does not preclude individual believers from combating abortion by legislative means or other such public engagement. Nor does it exclude the church's specific statements on such concrete matters as the restriction of religious liberty and other areas of concern that impinge on the spiritual mission of the church. These are not, however, the everyday activities of the church, lest the world misunderstands the church's role to be essentially and primarily political. Nor is there any reason to think the church can guarantee that in the final judgment the United States will be exempt from scrutiny.

It is astounding that the liberal media elite have viewed politically active conservative Christians as posing "a far greater threat to democracy than was presented by communism" (*The New York Times* editorial comment, "Government Is Not God's Work," Aug. 29, 1993). The editors deplore especially the Religious Right's insistence that religious values are a legitimate source of moral and political illumination rather than regarding such values as merely private prejudices. It slanders all who emphasize the relevance of religious values to the public sector to say they aim to create a theocracy or theonomy. Christian activists' real concern is to give as much public opportunity to promulgation of the gospel of Christ as secular humanists or atheists want for the advancement of their contrary views.

A Morally Vigilant Citizenry

Much media reaction has yet to discover what Tocqueville did over 150 years ago, that in the United States much of the nation's deep strength lies in a spiritually and morally vigilant citizenry. The ills of democracy are not due solely to the clamor of the underprivileged and to the confusion of the masses, but also to the cultural elite's tendency to deride and circumvent spiritual and moral dynamisms.

The insistence that private morality has no bearing on public fulfillment is reflective of a relativistic mania. A morally engaged citizenry will regard as culturally disintegrative an agenda that implies that human compassion gains its vitality from a fiscal redistribution by the government. Instead of championing limited government with mere lip service, an intellectually disciplined citizenry will promote responsible monetary policy, elimination of welfare fraud, and much else. It will reject the attempt to straightjacket religion into only private significance, and address the missing inner resources of character, in both its leaders and the masses, without which no form of government can confidently survive. Among the noblest features of the American heritage is the belief that leaders entrusted with public office should reflect standards of morality at least on a par with those of the citizenry they serve, and that they may even be expected to live in a manner exemplifying the nation's ideals.

The waning of self-control and community civility and public responsibility is in fact not unrelated to that "decay of religion" of which Lasch writes. Public virtue depends on private character, and private character emerges from convictions about the ultimately real world. It is a telling commentary that the United States rid itself of the Bible in public schools only to relocate policemen at their entrances to restrain violence. Major cities seem to be unified less by ethical commitments than by earthquake and flood, or by the victories of local sports teams. The muffling of primary doctrines such as sin and salvation encourages warped notions of "tolerance." Civic engagement cannot be revived in a society whose only absolutes are framed by self-interest and self-fulfillment. If every moral claim is adjusted to the priority of one's personal rights, no room remains for meaningful political conversation.

Democracy Beyond the Cold War

We live in a generation of immense upheaval, whose defining characteristics are so diverse that we cannot now be certain of some ultimate political outcomes. Surely that is true of Russia. A republic surrounded by presumably independent nations, Russia now has a democratic way of electing a president and parliament. Yet the development of democracy suffered a severe setback through Russia's brutal repression of Chechnia, and Yeltsin's unsure health and stance muddles the matter of national leadership. Presumably for defense and security, Russia reportedly has retained nuclear missiles along with some four thousand warheads which can be retargeted in "minutes' notice" should the cold war resume. Reportedly also it has retained the world's largest stockpile of chemical weapons. The dread possibility remains that the cold war in Eastern Europe may give way to a cold peace in an area beset as much with ethnic rivalries as with ideological conflict.

Gorbachev is the one transition figure without whom Russia's turn from totalitarianism toward democracy would not have been made, but he was unable to consolidate democratic forces. No guarantee exists that the former Soviet Marxist states will make the transition to democracy, and there are some fears that in Russia itself fascism may yet rise from the ashes of communism, or that some imperial state could reshape a great empire.

Has Democracy Had Its Day?

The aftermath of the cold war has yielded transitional problems almost as complicated as those posed by the cold war itself. Demands on the method and content of political change affect the confidence in democratic commitments. For many leaders, providing adequate levels of employment and containing runaway inflation are more important than human rights.

It seems likely that East Germany and probably Poland and an emerging Czech state will succeed as democracies. In Albania and Bulgaria the Marxist regimes have ended and terror no longer reigns, yet daily life is much the same as it was. In some former Soviet countries, Islam has a depth of support that could lead to dictatorships.

Casting out the Communist mind-set overnight is an inestimable ordeal. Long-established patterns do not vanish swiftly except through nondemocratic violence. Generational psychology shifts slowly in major transitions. When former Communists swiftly scoop up privatized properties, the capitalist model easily drifts into what Marx misconstrued it to be. Retired military officers, once-tenured academicians, and the now-displaced political literati who have lost former benefits are unsettling spirits in an already unstable society. In such circumstances it may take a half generation or longer for democracy to establish a firm root. What is true of Russia is true also of much of Eastern Europe.

China holds the key to Hong Kong, the world's third largest trading center. China's transition from communism is presently to an ambiguous, yet-to-be-defined alternative, held together less by law than by power, with strong bureaucrats resisting political change but promoting quite primitive economic reforms. Given the looming death of Deng Xiaoping, rival warlords and ambitious generals could either undermine national stability or promote a nationalist superpower. Defiance of human rights appeals indicates that, despite the masses' increasing disdain, the current regime's political liberalization is not prone to disavow Communist ideology.

At the same time, the remarkable economic transformation of Hong Kong, South Korea, Singapore, and Taiwan—and the parallel possibilities that may now dawn also among some Eastern European countries—signals the ability of free enterprise to sponsor massive changes. After coping long with Communist tyranny, Eastern European citizens now know the gratification of choosing one's vocation, of advancing according to one's skills, of being informed of world issues by a free press, of engaging aggressively in community affairs and supporting the political party of one's choice.

A Mixed Review

To see history whole, however, is to focus not only on politics and economics and military might and on freedom and its fortunes, but also on the corrupting influences of human power in both government and religion. The mounting carnage of contemporary civilization, its poverty of spirit and lust for material gain, calls for a spiritual down payment on what belongs neither to Caesar nor to Madison Avenue nor Wall Street.

Still, many good things can be said about American democracy. Tribute is voiced even by many who have yet to reap its full benefits. Some of the democracy's real allies are found among victims of poverty who seek to escape from welfare programs to a more conventional existence and normal life. We are unlikely to be reminded of national values by social critics who consider the United States the epicenter of the world's evils. Those who assail democracy from radical perspectives themselves avoid despair only by munching on facets of faith anchored in beliefs they now demean as outworn. Among the worst mistakes the friends of democracy can make is prematurely to abandon the silent needy.

An embattled multitude remains devoted to the biblical heritage despite secular society's routine underestimation of it. Most modern Christians view democracy favorably and believe it should be nurtured over against authoritarian governments. The surest way to lose it is to neglect its distinctives and to take it for granted.

American Evangelicals in the recent past have had serious reservations over both a politicized Protestantism and a politicized Catholicism, fearing a vigorous drive for religiopolitical power. The recent emergence of a largely politicized Evangelical movement has encouraged proposals for cooperative interreligious engagement in cobelligerency by coalitions sharing common moral and social concerns to arrest secular erosion of the nation's spiritual heritage.

Resistance or Renewal?

These developments thrust forward the question of acceptable political theory and activity. Granted that Christians should be more involved politically—possibly to the limit of their competence and opportunity—what type of engagement will comprise biblical obedience? Is it enough simply to resist the growing secularization of society, but with no more articulate vision than sporadic social and political participation that may influence society in competing ways? Should not serious reflection on the Christian philosophy of politics be an important aspect of thinking christianly?

The case for democracy is not limited to unequivocal opposition to totalitarian communism, commendable as that would be. Surely democratic principles must be clearly defined and strengthened. A political cadre that implies that whatever is legally permissible cannot be morally wrong, and that what is morally wrong is a matter of public indifference, poses a serious threat to a democratic society.

The goal of civic renewal must be not merely to repel democracy's assailants but also to restore the nation's foundations. This requires comprehensive effort. The connective tissue of a nation is neither democracy nor information or education. Every citizen must indeed have some understanding of democratic political processes, but he or she must also contribute in some personal way to the advancement of truth and justice.

Moral issues being raised today are not focused only on the margin of politics; the whole political enterprise is being cross-examined anew in the context of ethics. Justice and love are not merely matters of tolerance, especially not tolerance of evil. A revival of healthy democracy requires a clear voting majority, and, more importantly, a shared moral vision and purpose.

Out of this dynamic we are now seeing both family values and public economic responsibility again coming to the fore. There are some signs that illegitimacy is being restigmatized, and that the lost sense of shame is coming home again. Even some television shows seem to revive a distinction between right and wrong. "Feeling good" is being linked again to confession and repentance. Teenage pregnancy is eyed more critically. Hurried divorce evokes greater scrutiny, especially when children's lives are bartered.

We need to get beyond the growing impression that in a democracy the main duty of a president is to be reelected because if he is defeated he will cease to be president! The basic task of politicians is not to inspire enough monetary support to assure renomination.

More and more it is acknowledged that biblical and specifically Christian elements of religious faith had a significant impact upon early America. The United States may not have originated as a Christian government— indeed, the Founding Fathers disallowed a religious test for office—but there can be little doubt that the United States nevertheless was predominantly a Christian nation, that is, a geographical collectivity mainly of Christians.

No nation and no culture can long survive in the absence of shared values—indeed of transcendent values and absolutes. To speak meaningfully today of the invisible transcendent is to speak of the supernatural, self-revealing God of the Bible. All the speculative alternatives to the theistic creator and moral judge are collapsing into insignificance. Our highest ideals are not self-sustaining. Modernism and secular humanism are emptying into postmodernism with its denial of objective truth, objective good, and objective meaning.

The Priority of Freedom and Conscience

Nothing in Lord Acton's exposition of democracy is more impressive than his insistence on the priority of freedom and of conscience. To regard liberty and the moral sense merely

47

as speculative principles postulated at the expense of revealed religion is all too easy. To say that no presumption is valid against the conscience of mankind may be questionable indeed, especially if one insists, as Christians do, on transcendent revelation and on the moral fallenness of humanity. While conscience presently remains in need of correction, to act contrary to conscience is always wrong. A lively good conscience is among a citizenry's basic assets, for it will challenge ill-directed strivings for freedom that recognize no authority higher than the self, or the majority, or even the church and its related institutions. In brief, a good conscience contributes to the durability of democracy.

Freedom is revealed religion's supreme political promise and highest political end. Liberty requires the pursuit of an ideal civil society and the containment of arbitrary authority. During the American Revolution the clergy preached liberty—nothing less. They anticipated a day when humans would at last be free to choose the good and to do their duty, when liberty would be rescued from abuse by illicit authority and from the lust for power and possessions. It is a tenet of revealed religion that humans in their present condition are not free to do the good, although they may nonetheless fulfill civic duties and make moral choices.

The greatest text on freedom is that the truth—more particularly the redemption offered by the Son—sets one "free indeed" (John 8:32, 36). Abraham Lincoln spoke of "a new birth of freedom." Charles Malik, former chairman of the United Nations General Assembly, said that true freedom is the greatest promise that any nation can offer to the world, yet Western leaders now rarely talk about it.

True freedom is whole and, indivisible—it embraces political freedom, moral freedom, spiritual freedom, freedom of thought, freedom of belief, freedom of expression, free enterprise, a free press, free elections, but supremely, freedom to perform the will of God. Religious freedom is basic to all else; it offers humankind not only freedom not to worship Caesar, but freedom to worship Caesar's God, who is the ground of all human duties and rights.

One need not minimize economic concerns to emphasize that fiscal affairs by themselves are not adequate to preserve a democracy. Important as are issues such as budgetary balance and welfare costs, they must not obscure other moral and spiritual aspects of political debate. No government can perpetually survive on red ink, but without ethical imperatives it is unworthy of survival. Durable democracy includes among its corollaries a respect for private property and a free market. It affirms the role of law and human responsibility in all of cultural life. It affirms that rights exist prior to the state rather than being established by the state.

Revitalizing the Culture

A program of cultural revitalization will cope with secular society's displacement of religion without dismantling the Founding Fathers' insistence both on free expression and on nonestablishment. Yet no discussion of church and state affairs should ignore the fact that the church now needs repair as well as the government. Church growth is more than a numbers game; it involves holiness, neighbor-love, and a passion for justice. The church today needs more than periodic upgrading; it needs heart surgery and knee surgery.

Nonetheless, it is time for church-goers to take a rightful place in American society. Rejecting a reliance on political action alone as the sufficient remedy for social chaos does not provide grounds for abandoning civic concerns. Rather, it is a summons to a clearer understanding of both the indispensability and the limits of public policy. A cultural elite of humanists and other naturalists has sought to wall off religion from society and to contain it within private experience. If self-fulfillment becomes the supreme goal, materialism, hedonism and other isms will define this goal in conflicting ways. But no political agenda, however narrowly or broadly defined, can of itself adequately define the mind and will of a good society.

One's world view inevitably conditions one's behavior. Deep down, a comprehensive conception of the ultimately real world governs whether or not one ought to love one's neighbor as one's self, champion religious freedom, insist on private property, advance a free market rather than excessive government controls, or help risk-prone elements of society to recover human dignity. Such controlling convictions relate cognitively and volitionally to the Hebrews' confident awareness of a singular covenant-relationship to Yahweh and Christian insistence that the sinless, crucified Jesus rose bodily from the dead. To be sure, a free society gives one the liberty to either deny or affirm such beliefs, and even to dispense with religion. But religious disbelievers and believers alike must show the sources on which the categories of truth and justice and love finally turn.

Linked to the existence and reality of God—and not merely to majority opinion—are the issues of transcendent law, human equality, moral duty and future judgment, the family values of monogamy and fidelity, love of neighbor, and participation in community life on the side of justice. Belief in God is not mental enslavement, as communism asserted; it nurtures self-reliance and self-control through the divine source and ground of all true freedom.

The line between political action and what passes for gospel declaration has sometimes been extraordinarily thin. Those who justify political options by revelatory references alone readily appeal for theonomy, whereas others truncate public morality into private morality, forgetting that no government can simply turn the other cheek.

An appeal to natural law theory, insofar as it asserts a universally shared morality existing apart from divine disclosure, seems to run counter to the human condition. I do not believe that moral principles and political absolutes can be confidently formulated independently of divine revelation, contrary to natural law theorists' appeal to a "universal voice of reason." Although I affirm that politics must go beyond might and expediency to include moral principle and shared conscience, I am not persuaded (as Grotius was) that the principles of moral law would stand even if there were no God. There are indeed, as Grotius held, certain truths and principles by which states and their political interests stand or fall; society is held together by both hypothetical and real contracts. But these truths and principles are not demonstrable apart from the Christian doctrine of divine creation, the *imago Dei,* and the transcendently given Decalogue. The rejection of these truths and principles is related to humanity's fall and our ongoing moral rebellion. The creation-ethic reinforces and revises ethical imperatives through which the sullied but surviving *imago Dei* gains our attention.

However supremely Christians value revelatory, redemptive religion, we must beware nonetheless about hurriedly attaching Christian identity to specific legislative proposals such as a balanced-budget amendment or line-item veto. Devout Christians can disagree over specific political proposals or strategies, but they are assuredly doomed to irrelevance if they disagree about everything and do not identify the principles that govern their options. Deep generational issues turn, for example, on whether public schools should be shielded from religious values and from specifically biblical absolutes such as the Decalogue and the imperative of neighbor-love. Not only the direction of politics and education and science, but also the future of freedom itself, may well hinge on a decision over whether the Judeo-Christian heritage is to be checked at the door of the public classroom. If notable chapters of human progress remain to be written in the West, it is only persons of renewed moral focus and spiritual vitality that will stimulate them.

It is certainly possible that democracy may not be the wave of the future, despite the breakdown of Marxism. But world history bears trenchant testimony to the loss of liberty that has characterized nondemocratic societies. Among the options for modern society none is more practicable and promising than democracy, even though its gains may at times seem considerably less than impressive. When voluntarism gives way to compulsion, all fragile freedoms soon hang insecurely in the balances.

The Democratic Ideal

We must not overlook the fact that ideal democracy remains a dream that is found nowhere in reality. The United States stands at the threshold of a new millennium as the supreme world carrier of democratic principles. It has witnessed the collapse of the Soviet-totalitarian alternative. But America has far to go in fully actualizing democratic ideals of justice and compassion, equality and freedom. The American "experiment," for all its achievements, only imperfectly reflects its intended form. The United States can hardly be viewed as a mirror of democracy at its best. Before it emerges as a perfect reflection of democratic principles it will likely be overtaken by the final judgment of the nations. Nor is everything that occurs in a democracy compatible either with Christianity or even with democracy, as specters like radical individualism and materialistic greed attest. Democracy has in fact no built-in guarantee of permanent survival; its future in the next generation is tied to its effective preservation in the present. Yet no other human political program offers more rewarding possibilities of creative development through a displacement of dictatorial, authoritarian, and corrupt political institutions alongside the freedom to worship God in good conscience while promoting both justice for and love for neighbor.

For all its problems, the United States remains the most powerful and prosperous nation in history and the world's strongest force for democracy. While its human rights record is not unblemished, it has usually led the way among world powers. It has vigorously championed property rights, including intellectual rights. Its highly productive economy is nurtured by the creative free enterprise of corporate giants and entrepreneurial small business. Its record of religious freedom is impressive. It has counted resolutely for world peace, even while its own citizenry has divided at times on the issue of political self-interest. It remains a refuge of hope on the political horizon; it is the nation to which the world's underprivileged constantly seek to repair. Were it to vanish suddenly from the globe, the remnants of the Free World would be plunged into grief and mourning.

Yet the entire political enterprise is in need of critical and constructive evaluation, including the ability of monied citizens to propel themselves into the political forefront, the size and influence of campaign contributions, and the acceptance of gifts by already well-salaried officeholders.

To clarify its vision, the United States requires more than all else an end-of-the-century formulation of national purpose. Although it has in the recent past heavily funded many world peacekeeping missions, it cannot forever go into all the world bent on global nation-building and perpetual peacekeeping.

The Western political alliance, which has maintained peace in Europe, seems more and more to lack solidarity and conviction. Foreign policy specialists and political leaders seem increasingly divided in respect to intervention in international disputes and military eruptions. The future of the U.N., the future of NATO, even the future of the American-European alliance are increasingly in debate. The regrets of some national leaders over Vietnam, the unanticipated consequences in Somalia, and the frustrating stalemate in Bosnia make the United States as the leading world power seem confused even to its allies.

Democracy itself stands at a decisive crossroads in a watershed moment of world history. It is the champion of political freedom and equality in a world of bondage and conflict, yet it can fulfill its highest promise only through the transcendent realities that Christianity affirms.

A Resurgent Conscience

Fifty years ago in the United States the lethargic conscience of American fundamentalism became uneasy over its virtual abandonment to Modernism of the culture of a novel democratic nation founded mainly by freedom-loving Christians. A spiritual resurgence stretching across five decades has nurtured a global Evangelical movement making unparalleled gains in evangelism and world mission, in Christian philanthropy and church growth, in private college and seminary education, and in publication of religious books and magazines.

At mid-century the fundamentalist-evangelical witness was largely locked out of modernist American culture through its own deliberate concentration on a mission of personal regeneration; now a half century later it is indecisively trapped between escape from a culture dominated by humanistic-naturalistic controls and the discomfiting realization that only an overwhelming spiritual renewal and a massive transcendent penetration of the social order can effectively challenge and preserve a rapidly disintegrating society.

Exploring Cobelligerency

For the preservation of Judeo-Christian values, now largely marginalized by a social order whose distinctives secular humanism currently defines, Evangelicals may well need to venture a heretofore unthinkable alliance with Roman Catholics, historically their theological and ecclesiastical rivals. Catholics likewise cannot decisively reshape the political arena without Evangelical cobelligerency.

To such an effort Catholics and Evangelicals bring not only noteworthy commonalities but separate and differing perspectives and distinctives as well. A sophisticated network of Catholic scholars champions the natural law theory of Thomas Aquinas and the political philosophy of John Courtney Murray in pursuit of a so-called "common good." This supports the impression of a widely shared Catholic public philosophy, although many traditional Catholics consider democracy, with its insistence on church-state separation and on pluralistic political participation, unacceptable except perhaps for interim or pragmatic purposes. Evangelicals, on the other hand, reflect a diversity of public philosophies; some have none at all. Many of them, moreover, consider Roman Catholics the proper objects of New Testament evangelism more than as partners in a common political engagement.

The success of any effort to arrest current social deterioration and regain a cultural initiative for biblical values may well depend upon an ability to transcend governing differences for limited ends. The risks of a miscarriage of expectations in a carefully honed theological-cultural alliance, if not ventured, may be outweighed by the social deterioration to postmodernism that threatens to eclipse the entire spiritual and moral inheritance of the West.

Precisely the depth of the current social crisis may present a new and urgent opportunity for Evangelicals and Catholics to discuss their historic differences in quest of some larger fulfillment of the long-forfeited unity of the churches. Evangelicals are widely committed to Reformation theology and are hostile to papal Christianity; they are aware, moreover, that a relaxation of church and state separation may drive secular culture to even deeper hostility to the transcendent—or lead ultimately to a revival of church-state patterns that early Americans eagerly escaped. Yet more than an uneasy conscience, it is a deeply unsettled spirit that troubles many Evangelicals. They are faced by a culture markedly worse than that deplored by fundamentalism a half century ago, yet one which the evangelical resurgence has only sporadically and fragmentarily addressed.

It would be supreme irony if the plight of democracy were elevated to crisis dimensions not only by moral ambiguity and religious privatization but also by a confused Christian response to the political dimensions of the culture conflict. Could it be that Christianity's historic divisions might play themselves out in terms of weak or divided support for the essentials of the democratic process and thus contribute unwittingly to its demolition? Because they espoused too narrow an agenda, Evangelicals already have missed major opportunities to repair the ailments of democracy, despite the rise of the Moral Majority, the Religious Right, the Christian Coalition, and other agencies that have helped identify a substantial bloc of citizens whose loyalties to the Judeo-Christian heritage are firm. In a two-party system something is to be said, moreover, for the wisdom of the church not making an unqualified Christian commitment to any one political party for much more than one day at a time.

Democracy, to be sure, is not Christianity; a vote for democracy is not a vote either for papal Catholicism or for Reformational Protestantism. Democracy is a political process that champions religious liberty and sustains an atmosphere in which voluntary religion can thrive. Its effective survival is rendered problematical when religion and morality—its twin supports—themselves become part of the problem rather than allies in a proffered solution. Should democracy collapse, Christianity can and will survive. But it will be high cultural tragedy if the Christian elements of society, through their disunity and unresolved differences, reflect negatively both on democracy and on the community of faith and imply the irrelevance of Christian impact during a decisive turning of the cultural tide.

A program of political cobelligerency need not imply theological identity. It can be ventured at some points even with non-Christians. We should not hesitate to join even with humanists on specific issues where their otherwise controversial social agenda may be acceptable, even though their ontology and epistemology are very different from ours, and humanists cannot make an unassailable case on their speculative premises. In the political arena there are issues on which not only Evangelicals and Catholics and Greek Orthodox agree, but also Mormons and Muslims, and we should stand for the right in a political context that insists on human freedom and equality. The state is not to be an arbiter of metaphysical validity.

In our shared recognition of the great ecumenical creeds, Evangelicals can find with Roman Catholics and Orthodox believers a deeper motivation for public cooperation, one that lies in our mutual dedication to Judeo-Christian values. We live amid a permissive and relativistic generation that strives to legalize its preferred alternatives while it disdains the inherited ethic as a cultic imposition. Respect for the teaching of sacred Scripture, for truth and the good, for human liberty and dignity, for the laws of logic, and for new life in the Spirit and neighbor-love and social justice, are concerns that remain divine imperatives, whether or not a rebellious contemporary society reaches for a divinely assured future. The prospect of peace on earth and global justice is in the Bible messianically grounded because of divine grace and the sinful human condition. No literate Christian will obscure that referent unless he considers revealed religion but a wistful echo of the past rather than an ongoing hope.

Still we must ask whether the formation of a Catholic Party or an Evangelical Party or even a Christian Coalition is the most prudent way to engage in political involvement.

The role of the clergy can be confusing in the matter of cobelligerency, since they are mainly the theological specialists who stand in the background—if not in the foreground—of official interdenominational and inter-church dialogue. They are moreover often indirectly decisive of the outcome of conferences and symposiums by suggesting invited and disinvited personnel. In this way dialogue often advances a hidden agenda. The recent

Catholic-Evangelical Statement, for example, alienated numbers of its potential supporters who were not prepared for all its affirmations, objected to others because of ambiguous phrasing, and thought still other concerns should have been mentioned.

Such factors would argue for a two-track dialogue that carefully preserves a distinction of political and theological concerns. Nothing is more confusing in doctrinal discussions than when one of the participants congenially comments that he/she does not personally subscribe to an officially espoused view, since the debate is not over private orthodoxy but the acceptability of authoritative tradition or established church order. It is important that technical theologians participate, that the issues at stake be formulated authoritatively, and that the dialogue pointedly engages the disputed concerns. In this way the political crisis facing democracy can at the same time be a stimulus to theological renewal, one that would assign to the truth of revelation the priority it deserves. If political collegiality is ultimately prized above theological consensus, the wrong priority prevails. Supposedly in the name of civilizational rescue, we repeat the error of confused priorities that has precipitated and contributed to the existing cultural decline.

Holding High "The Truth"

The task of the churches is not the task of government. We are not to insist on doctrinal conformity as a condition of political cooperation, or to insist that political cooperation is presently more important and urgent than theological precision and consensus. The Christian can welcome political pluralism in a fallen society, but knows full well that heaven and the regenerate church have a much stricter theological norm. The identification of that norm is a task that falls to evangelism and to civic dialogue, not to legislation and compulsion. Yet its neglect and evasion by the citizenry carries devastating consequences, so that Christians do their contemporaries high disservice if they do not publish the standards by which humans and nations will, in their view, be finally judged.

61

Has Democracy Had Its Day?

The detachment of law from transcendent revelation and its attachment instead to secular humanism and to naturalistic relativism has unraveled the moral fabric of the nation. Whereas the founders of the Republic spoke of self-evident truths, the oncoming generation is encouraged by its mentors not only to question any truth's self-evidence, but whether truth exists at all. Society has "progressed" in 2,500 years to a resurrection of the biases of the ancient Greek Sophists.

To exhibit again the truths and ethical absolutes of revealed religion—not least of all that Jesus Christ is "the truth"—and define the public behavior this implies for a secular culture that has reached a moral dead end, and to do so compatibly with democratic principles, is now our demanding task. If we succeed in this task, the once-familiar lyrics of "The Star Spangled Banner" will sound forth again from a "heav'n rescued land" in praise of "the Pow'r"—not merely economic and military—"that hath made and preserved us a nation."

Summarized as an Acton Institute lecture given in Grand Rapids, Michigan, on Tuesday evening, November 7, 1995.

About the Author

Carl F.H. Henry has had a distinguished career as a writer, editor, and teacher among Evangelical Christians. He began his academic career at Wheaton College, where he earned B.A. and M.A. degrees, followed by a Th.D. from Northern Baptist Theological Seminary in Chicago and a Ph.D. from Boston University. He is probably most widely known for his twelve-year tenure as the first editor of *Christianity Today* magazine and another nine years as editor-at-large. His writings include *The Uneasy Conscience of Modern Fundamentalism*, one of his early works (1948) cited in this book; the six-volume *God, Revelation and Authority* (1983); and, more recently, *Toward a Recovery of Christian Belief* (1990). For several years he taught on the faculty of Northern Baptist Theological Seminary and then Fuller Theological Seminary, Pasadena, Calif. He has lectured or served as visiting professor in schools across the United States and on virtually every continent. Among his honors are awards from the Freedoms Foundation and the American Heritage Foundation.